Money and Bitcoin:
Everything You Were Never Taught In School

Jay Dyer

Money and Bitcoin: *Everything You Were Never Taught In School*

Copyright © 2021, by Jay Dyer.

Edited by:

Johnnie Goolsby, Lisa Carr, and Alanda Dyer.

ISBN: 978-1-7366415-1-4

Dedication

To my late mother, Ruth Miller...
She dedicated her life to making sure she was
the most responsible, self-sufficient, moral, and
honorable example of how to live life.
I learned a lot from your example.
To my wife, Alanda...
Thank you for your support and patience.
To my grandchildren...
Richard, Antheny, Malichi, and Thomas.
Finally, to my great-grandson, Hunter.
I can't be a part of your lives.
So, I pass this knowledge on to each of you the
only way I can think of.
I pray it helps you protect your futures.

Jay Dyer

Table of Contents

Preface

Money is arguably the most important outside influencer in our day-to-day lives. There is never a day when we do not spend money in one form or another. Even if you are homeless, you use or consume something that costs you or someone else money. Money and/or the lack thereof, influences or dictates some, if not all of our activities.

In this book I will tell you who, what, when, and why — then offer solutions to it all. Don't make the mistake of jumping to the solutions. Without knowing the what, when, and why, the solution will make no sense to you. It's like someone telling you the ultimate answer is 7. Okay??? What was the question, and why did it need to be asked? Funny thing, no one seems to know much about money.

We all know we need it. We work for it, people die in the pursuit of it, and without it, some people fear living. Without it, many die. Yet, when some ask, "Why is it the harder I work, the less I seem to have?" or, "Why do I feel like the more I have, the more I need?"

No one seems to ever have a satisfactory answer. In this book, I'm going to explain the mess we are in, how we got into it, who did it to us, and what we can do about it.

For the first time in the history of mankind, we, the people of Planet Earth, have a choice — and the power — to do something about who or what controls money.

I want everyone reading this book to question everything I'm writing. The main purpose for my writing is to inspire you to LEARN for yourself. I don't want you to buy anything, join anything, protest, or support anything. I want you to protect yourself and your family with knowledge.

Knowledge is power; I call those who are the last to learn victims. I'm writing this book to inform, enlighten, and provoke thought. I will not be providing references nor sources. I want you to investigate and prove me wrong.

One last thing before I begin: I don't give a rat's ass about being politically correct. If you chose to get offended by the words I use instead of hearing the important meaning of what I have to say, then that's on you. I'll begin with a short history of money.

If you'd like to learn the full story, read "The Creature from Jekyll Island" and "The History of Money and Banking in the United States."

You can also watch the series "The Hidden Secrets of Money" on YouTube. What I'm sharing is not limited to the USA. In fact, it is the story of money around the world. What I hope to do is break things down and explain in everyday simple terms not only what happened, but how you are personally affected by it.

Before we start down this road, we must have a common understanding of how I use certain words. While it may seem unnecessary to some, I would feel more confident we would all arrive at the same destination if we have the same understanding of these words.

You don't have to agree with my definitions, you just need to understand how I'm using the words.

Glossary

Money: Any store of value two people agree to use in order to trade goods and services between one another. Traits of money: portable, recognizable, durable, divisible, and scarce.

Currency: Anything other than money two or more people agree represents money and can be used in its place. Traits of currency: portable, recognizable, and divisible.

Fiat: Something whose value or power can be given or withdrawn by an issuing authority. Only people who respect and honor the issuer's authority will honor its proclaimed value. Example: You can't use a ticket to the football game at the baseball game even if they are on the same date and time.

The ticket has no value on its own. Its temporary value is fiat, declared by those organizing the football game and has no value to those organizing the baseball game. Anything that has value only as long as the power behind it supports it, has fiat value.

Purchasing Power: An agreed upon amount of goods and/or services that can be traded for a specific amount of money or currency.

Value: The amount of purchasing power a unit of money or currency has. Value is always relative to or pertaining to purchasing power.

Inflation: The process of reducing the purchasing power of each unit of a currency by increasing the amount of that currency faster than the growth of the population it services. Too much money chasing a few goods causes the price of the goods to go up.

Deflation: The process of increasing the amount of purchasing power for each unit of currency through the reduction of the amount of currency that services a set or growing number of people.

A stable supply of currency that services an ever-increasing number of people or a combination of both. Example: Gold and dollars service the world population as stores of value. There are many more dollars than ounces of gold. Each dollar has less purchasing power than each ounce of gold.

As the total number of dollars increases relative to the total number of ounces of gold, the purchasing power of dollars goes down and the purchasing power of gold, in terms of dollars, goes up. This causes gold to deflate and dollars to inflate.

The Banks: Owners and beneficiaries of the institutions.

Supply and Demand: Having more people after less goods makes each good more expensive. Having more goods than people who want them, makes each good less expensive.

Being the only supplier of a good that is needed, will allow you to charge more for that good. Being the only supplier of a good no one wants means your good is worthless. In supply and demand, services are classified as a good. Supply and demand are the driving forces that determine the current value of any inflating or deflating commodity.

Interest: A fee (profit or debt) charged for the use of money lent/borrowed. For lenders, the amount of profit you charge for the use of your money by someone you lend it to. For borrowers, the amount of additional debt you owe over and above the amount of money you borrowed. In a debt-based economy, interest by definition is an inflationary instrument; it creates new money that did not exist before the loan.

In a deflationary economy, interest CANNOT exist. If it does, it becomes a counter agent instrument, making all money before the loan MORE valuable.

Ignorant: Possessing a LACK of knowledge. Operating or making decisions without the most important facts. Example: A baby or child runs into the street without looking both ways. Or a child that sticks a knife into an electrical socket for the first time. Ignorant.

Stupid: Not acting in your best interest while having the necessary knowledge to make better choices. Example: A normal adult—who for no good reason— walks/runs into the street without looking both ways.

Or anyone who sticks a knife into a working electrical socket for the second time, after being shocked the first time. Stupid.

Fool: A person who does not learn from past mistakes or, who continues down a path they know will hurt them. Example: Anyone that sticks a knife into a working electrical socket more than twice. Fool.

Idiot: Someone who wants to follow, imitate, or become like a known fool.

Or anyone who refuses to hear or consider any information that is contrary to their personal beliefs for no other reason than it is not what they believe. Idiot.

Ponzi Scheme: A process that takes money invested by later investors to pay profits to earlier investors.

The largest legal Ponzi scheme is Social Security. Workers today are paying into a system as an investment for their future, while the money paid into the system today goes directly to retired workers of yesteryear.

When the number of new workers paying into the system becomes too few to support the payments to current retirees, the system must be funded from other sources or it collapses.

Chapter 1

Ignorance is Bliss

Most people are living their financial lives in near total ignorance. The basics of what money is, and how it works are subjects almost no one is taught in school. Economics is a subject reserved for nerds. Those who chose to become accountants and economists are almost as far down on the ladder of popularity as you can go and still be on the ladder.

It's no wonder that when the subject of money comes up, if you aren't telling someone where or how they can get some, they have little to no interest in what you're babbling about. This is not by accident. Our society has been designed to keep as many people ignorant as can be on this subject.

For example: Were you taught in school, or by your parents, or by anyone as a child what money is, and how, why, and when new money is created? Were you taught the difference between money and currency?

Did anyone ever mention to you how to turn currency into money or why you should do so? Has anyone ever explained why money is better than currency or when to use each one? Did anyone in your life explain how holding onto currency can cost you money? Did anyone ever explain how you could make $200,000 a year and still be POOR?

I can go on and on. The vast majority of you will have answered NO to all of those questions. If so, you are living your life in financial ignorance. Believe me, it is NOT your fault. While writing this, I am 67 years old and until three years ago I lived as you are now, in complete ignorance. I didn't have a clue. I thought working hard, saving money, and investing what I could was the way to provide for myself and my family — WRONG!

Did you know people who use a credit card to make a purchase when they have the money for such items in the bank or in their pockets are doing so because they are ignorant of how money works? If they are doing so, and they do know how money works, keep reading to find out why now, I'd call those people stupid. The first thing I had to learn and recognize was real money and how it differed from currency.

Chapter 2

Real Money vs Currency

The year was 1970, I was 18. My mother wanted to buy another house. The three-bedroom house we lived in throughout my junior high and high school years had just been stolen by the city of Los Angeles, under the guise of Imminent Domain.

For $15,000 we lost our home so the Century Freeway could be built. Side note: The reason I say stolen is the project did not start construction until fifteen years after the purchase. Smart for the city, bad for us.

We looked in several areas and we found a nice, four-bedroom, two-story home in San Dimas, CA. That home was selling for $26,400. My mom turned the house down because 26K was way too much money at that time. Her mortgage payments at 8.5% would have been over $250 a month. In her eyes, she just couldn't afford it. Now, today that same house cost $585,000. In hindsight, you wonder, what was she thinking?

Everyone today thinks she made a terrible mistake. Yes, in U.S. dollars she made an absolutely horrible financial decision. Who wouldn't struggle to make a $250 payment to have a house worth over half a million dollars from just $26,400?

Well as it turns out, she made a smart decision IF we were talking about paying for the house in full with real money.

This would have been my mother's third house. She saved up and paid cash in full for the previous two. The thought of 30 years of payments frightened her. If she had bought the house, let's look at this purchase from two different points of view.

First, we'll do the math for seeing how she would have fared using the U.S. dollar currency. It's simple: The current price of $585,000 divided by the original price, $26,400 means she would have made 22.159 times her investment in the house.

Who wouldn't go for a deal like that? Yes, the American dream come true. Now let's look at the same purchase using a real money like gold.

At that time, gold was selling for $35 per ounce. So, if we divide the cost of the house then, ($26,400) by the cost of an ounce of gold ($35), we see that   she would have needed just a little over 754 ounces of gold to buy the house. Now let's see the value in real money today.

Gold is about $1,350 per ounce. So, again let's divide the current cost of the house by the cost of an ounce of gold. That's 585,000 divided by 1,350 = 433.33. Today the house would only cost a little over 433 ounces of gold. That's a LOSS of 321 ounces of gold. The house today is only worth a little over HALF the gold it cost in 1970. She made the smart move even if she didn't know it.

Chapter 3

Purchasing Power

The moral of the story is that real money gets more valuable the longer you have it and currency gets less valuable the longer you have it. Let's think about it for a minute or two more. Using the amounts in the story above: Say we have two people, one with gold the other with cash, each with $26,400 in 1970. The one, with cash, buys the house above, the other buries the 754 ounces of gold in his backyard, or puts it in a bank safety deposit box. In 2019 they both get values on their property at the same time. The person with gold would have $433,350 MORE purchasing power or value, than the person who bought the house.

Here's the math on that. The equivalent of 754 ounces was paid for the house. The house's current value is 433 ounces. That's a loss of 321 ounces. 321 times 1,350 (todays per ounce price of gold) is 433,350. Just to hit the nail on the head again, the current value of 754 ounces of gold is $1,017,900.

The current value of the house is $585,000. The house lost value compared to gold. However, buying the house still would have been a great deal even with the loss. Here's why...

Let's suppose one person had gold and the other had cash in U.S. dollars. Both people put their money in a safety deposit box or buried the money at the same time, again, in 1970. The one with gold would have $1,017,900 of purchasing power today. That is 38.55 times its original dollar value. While the one that buried $26,400 in cash only has $26,400 in today's U.S. dollar purchasing power. In today's dollars that is 26,400 divided by 1,017,900, equals 0.0259% of the original 1970 purchasing power.

Did that wake you up? That is over 99.974% LOSS in purchasing power. Buying the house gave the person a place to live and preserved some of his purchasing power. Holding onto cash for long periods of time is NEVER a good idea in our current system. All the examples above demonstrate the difference between a real store of value (money and property), and currency that just represents money. Money maintains value, currency loses value by design. The design element in this process is called inflation.

Chapter 4

Inflation and the Rule of 72

Every economist in the world will tell you that 2-3% inflation is needed for a healthy economy and monetary system to grow and flourish. Anyone who knows the Rule of 72 understands 2% inflation means your currency losses half its value every 35.5 years.

The Rule of 72 says: divide 72 by any interest rate and the answer is the amount of time it will take for your currency to double. In the case of inflation, it is the amount of time it will take to lose half its value.

When have you known the U.S. or the world economy to exist on less than 2% inflation for any length of time? In fact, most of the time, the average inflation rate has been in the area of 4-6%. So, the currency supply and your purchasing power gets cut in half every 12 to 18 years. The Rule of 72 is a double-edged blade.

It is used by you to let you know how fast your investments will grow; it is used by the banks to determine how fast their profits will grow. Here's the difference: the interest rate you get on your savings and investments might be in the neighborhood of 2-7% if you're lucky.

That means at most, your investments double every 10 to 35 years. When you borrow money, for any purpose except a home purchase, the interest rate you pay is normally anywhere from 7-29%. That means the bank doubles it's money, and you pay twice what you borrowed every two to 10 years.

Do the math on your own credit cards and loans. It does not matter how much you owe. What matters is how long it takes you to repay. As you will see when you get to Chapter 6, the bank makes tons of profit when it lends you money. If you were to loan money to people and charge the same interest rate as banks, you would be in danger of being arrested as a loan shark. I mentioned that home loans are a bit different. While the Rule of 72 still applies, other factors come into play to increase the bank's earnings.

Adding bank fees on the loan as well as other service charges combined with the time you'll take to pay off a home loan, say 30 years, you will have paid the bank at least 2.5 to 3.5 times the original price of the home.

That means, that if the home does not increase in value over that same amount of time to more than 3.5 times its original price, you have lost money.

So, let's say your home cost you $230,000 and 30 years later you sell it for $500,000. You still lost approximately $305,000 because 3.5 x 230000 = 805000, which is what you've paid over that period of time.

The bank would say you lived in the house and you must pay someone for that utility. I say wrong! If you were able (and I understand most people are not) to pay cash for the home, whatever increase in value the home develops over the years would be profit for you.

Instead, you've paid the bank more profit over the years than the house has generated. Most, if not all of that natural value growth instantly becomes profit for the banks. Let's look at this math...

Your home cost $230,000. If you had no interest and you paid it off over 30 years, it would cost you $7,833 per year. That is $653 per month. We all know that would never happen.

But if it did, you'd be paying $653 per month directly to the principal of the loan. Instead, at 4% interest you are paying $395,300 for the house, of which $165,300 is interest and your monthly payment is $1098. But a funny thing happens here.

Instead of the whole $653 going to principal and the rest going to interest, the opposite happens. $405 goes to principal and $653 goes to interest. The next month the interest is calculated on the remaining balance.

If the bank calculated the payments the way normal people would, the principal would go down faster because the larger amount would be applied to the principal each month. Amortized loans pay far less to the principal in the beginning of the loan and much more to the principal at the end of the loan.

This is because the banks know most people don't stay in a home for more than 10 years before moving or refinancing.

So, by applying most of your payments to interest in the beginning, they make many times more profit over the average mortgage life span. But it gets worse.

Now let's imagine you've lived in the house for five years. The house has gone up in value to $400,000 and interest rates for new loans is now 2%. You decide to refinance to the lower interest rate and pull $50,000 cash out to add a new room onto the house.

Here is what you have just done to yourself: five years of paying on your home has reduced the principal by only $24,300. You have paid $39,180 in interest. With your new loan, you are starting over for 30 more years. The $63,480 you've paid has gone bye-bye, straight into the bank's pocket. You now owe $255,700. That's more than the original purchase price.

So, to recap, you've paid $63,480, you are $25,700 more in debt than when you started, and you still have 30 years to pay on this debt at a new monthly cost of $945. That means over the span of 35 years, you will have paid a total of $403,680, but only IF you are NEVER a day LATE on a payment and never refinance again.

Chapter 5

Credit and Savings

My next two statements are harsh but true. First, using credit is stupid except in very rare cases. Second, long-term savings are stupid and should very rarely be done.

So, if you shouldn't borrow and you shouldn't save, how are you supposed to buy anything you don't have the money for? The short answer is, most of the time, you shouldn't. Let me explain.

Remember my definition of inflation? Later, you'll learn that when you use a credit card or take out a loan for anything that does not return or make you more money than the loan, you are just adding to inflation and diluting the money supply.

In other words, you are making every dollar you have now, or get in the future, worth less. Using a CREDIT card to buy groceries, fast food, TVs, appliances, and the like, rob any savings and/or future currency of its purchasing power.

You will see and hopefully understand how this works later. Some would ask: If I pay off my charges within the first 30 days and no interest is charged, how am I adding to inflation?

It's simple; even if you pay the loan back right away, the currency that was transferred to the vendor was still new currency that did not exist before you made the purchase. Credit limits are NOT currency held on account for you, like currency you deposited in the bank.

Your credit limit is a limit on the amount of currency they are willing to CREATE on your behalf. It is currency created out of thin air, that once transferred from your account to the vendor, becomes a debt to you, and an asset for the bank; and once deposited in the bank by the vendor, it becomes the basis for the bank to grant new loans.

This too will be explained later. Let us not forget the interest, if charged, is instant profit for the bank and a debt for you as well.

As you repay the debt and interest, your payments/deposits are used as a basis for new loans, and it becomes a part of the currency supply. Thereby increasing and completing another step in the inflationary cycle.

To recap: both your borrowing and repayment, along with the deposits from the vendors you purchased from, become the foundation for more bank loans and profits plus adding to the rate of inflation.

Chapter 6

You're Paying Too Much

When you use a credit card for normal purchases, you are also paying too much. Think of it like volunteering to pay three or more times the sticker price for everything you buy. Let's say you want to purchase a new TV that costs $300. If you were to pay for the TV out of your pocket, it would cost you $300 plus tax. By paying with a credit card, you will — if you're like most people — pay at least $630 to $1,470 for that $300 TV. Some, a very few, people pay off their credit cards every month.

Think back. Are you one of those people? Most are not. Most people pay minimum payments each month. Which means that charge takes from 3 to 7 years to pay off. Think about paying $17.50/month at a 17-29% interest rate; that's $630 to $1,470 over the life of the repayment period.

Remember the Rule of 72? It works the opposite for the bank. Dividing 72 by the interest rate now tells you how short a time it will take for the bank to DOUBLE its money.

If you didn't do it when I asked you to in Chapter 4, try it now with the interest rate on any of your credit cards. That number tells you how long it will take for you to OWE and REPAY the bank twice as much as you borrowed.

Keep in mind, that's if you only have the ONE charge on your card. Nobody does that. Most are charging multiple items. It gets to the point people max out the card and can only make the minimum payments just to keep up. Does this sound familiar? Credit card companies LOVE SUCKERS like us. Not only do we make minimum payments but sometimes we are late, and that gives the bank an excuse to add late fees and raise the interest rate — making them even more profit.

People, think! Would you still buy that TV if the salesperson said, "You can pay $300 today or pay $1,470 over time."

Here is the bad part. No salesperson will ever tell you that because they don't get the extra money. The company that's selling you the TV will get $300 plus tax from the bank. The bank will collect from $330 to $1,470 in pure profit, all from you. ON JUST ONE PURCHASE!

Chapter 7

They Know What They Are Doing

Banks market to everyone that anything can be yours now for a low monthly payment. The store wants to make a sale. The salesperson does not care that you buying something on credit will inflate all their future money. They only care about making the sales commission now.

Economists tell us the economy must grow at a steady pace of 1-2% inflation per year. What they don't tell you is, the bank is the only winner in an inflationary economy.

When it comes to credit or cash payments, the bank gets a cut of every purchase. If all currency spent must first go through or end up in the bank, the bank makes profit each time currency moves.

That means the bank must keep currency flowing at a steady pace to keep their balance sheets showing more profit each year.

◆ ◆ ◆

If you simply saved for the TV or put it on layaway, you'd have from $330 to $1,470 more to spend on you or your family.

In this case, saving is a good thing. It's good because you are saving for a short time and spending the currency before it has time to lose purchasing power. Short-term savings can be a great vehicle to getting things for vanity or pleasure.

What about long-term savings? Things like retirement, end of life cost, college tuition and the like – why do I say this type of saving is stupid? That's because of a little thing called inflation.

Because inflation varies from 1-9% each year, it is IMPOSSIBLE for your savings to maintain its original purchasing power unless it grows more than 2-10% each year. For savings to grow in value, they must grow more and faster than the rate of inflation. Banks today are paying 0.01% interest per YEAR. So, simple math will tell you that you are losing the rate of inflation in purchasing power each year you save currency.

Banks have you convinced you must give all your savings to them to invest, in order to earn enough interest to outpace inflation each year. The problem is all the currency you place in the bank for them to invest, is just more currency the bank can lend on.

This ever-widening cycle of deposits, and loans, causes inflation growth year after year. This makes it next to impossible for your money to grow fast enough to support you when you are older.

Chapter 7a

Here Is How They Fool You

Yes, on the surface it looks like you are gaining. Each year, it seems that you have more money saved. The balance keeps getting larger and larger. There's only one problem: the purchasing power of that currency is shrinking faster than the number of dollars is raising.

It really makes no sense to start out with $100 and ten years later you have $500, if that $500 will only purchase what $75 of the original $100 would purchase. You've wasted ten years saving/investing and still lost $25 in value.

Most don't notice this because they now have $500, when they started with $100. It's not how much currency you have that matters, it's how much can you purchase with that amount of currency. Credit and inflation destroys purchasing power. They rob you of what you work so hard for. Bankers have fooled everyone in the middle and lower classes into thinking there is no other way to protect the future except to work hard, save, invest, and maintain a high credit score.

They want you to do this only with their help. All the while making it next to impossible to save or invest effectively.

Chapter 8

Bankers Created A New Business

With inflation causing prices to rise, salaries staying stagnant, and the stock market being manipulated by the banks themselves, it's no wonder it takes two or three wage earners to perform as well as one wage earner from the 1950s or 1960s.

Do you wonder how we, as a world, find ourselves in this situation? Don't worry, not many do. It's just not something that crosses the mind of the average person. "It is what it is," or "During inflation, things go up," seems to be what most reply when asked this question.

Most ask, "Why think about something you can't change?" Here's a short version of how we came to be where we are. Don't make the mistake of skipping this. Without this information, the rest of the book and the solutions won't make any sense.

In the beginning banks were created for NO other reason than to safeguard people's money.

Kings, governments, noblemen, and eventually regular people would deposit gold and silver in the bank for SAFEKEEPING. Bankers would issue a script stating how much value was deposited. People started passing around the script (banknotes) as payments. People taking the banknotes would also pay for goods and services with them.

Over time the banknotes became "good as gold" because everyone knew the gold was safe in the bank. Not too long after, bankers realized they were keeping gold and silver that people were not claiming. They also noticed that people were using their banknotes as currency.

Bankers decided to start loaning banknotes (currency) based on the gold and silver they had in their vaults. With the owner's permission and a promise to pay them part of the interest, bank-loaning, customer-backed currency was born. That went extremely well, as both parties profited through interest charges.

Customers, bankers, and loan recipients were all very happy. Then bankers said to themselves, "No one will know if we begin to lend more currency than we actually have."

So, they tried it, and it too was a success. That less than honest technique seemed to also stimulate the local economy. Everyone had currency to spread around. After a while, people got wind of how little tangible money the banks had on hand and some started turning in their banknotes. When banks ran out of real money to return, people panicked. Banks closed early and there was rioting in the streets.

Now you'd think the police would march right down to the banks and arrest the bank officers for fraud. After all, they were loaning money they did not have and charging interest for something that did not exist. Bankers were not jailed. Instead, bankers used their money, influence, and political power to trick the government into letting banks control money altogether.

In 1913, Congress was duped into establishing the Federal Reserve Bank (the FED) and what became the Internal Revenue Service. The bill, passed while most of congress was home for Christmas, basically said the FED would supply (loan) currency whenever the government needed it and the IRS would be responsible for enforcing collections of income taxes to repay the currency the government borrowed. In case you missed it, there was no permanent income tax or IRS before 1913.

Before 1913, these were temporary tools used mostly to fund war. A group of bankers wrote this bill secretly on Jekyll Island then tricked/convinced Congress to make these tools permanent. By passing the bill, the government-sanctioned banks to continue this fraud. In doing so, the government alluded that as long as banks kept writing checks whenever the government needed them, and banks kept at least 10% of what people deposit available to the people, the government will insure banks against loss for the other 90% of created, fake money.

That was the start of modern, bank-caused inflation. This process has a name, Fractional Reserve Lending. All that means is the bank must keep a fraction of each deposit as a reserve to service customers who want real money. You must remember, at that time, real money was gold and silver.

Chapter 9

Fractional Reserve Lending

Let's look at this process using numbers so you can see what is really happening here. For the sake of this story, there is only one bank in a small town. John deposits $100 in the bank.

The bank loans $90 to Sam. Sam spends the $90 to get his roof fixed. The roofer deposits the $90 in the bank, then they lend out $81 to Bob. Bob spends the currency on new clothes and the store owner deposits the currency back into the bank.

The bank then lends $71.90 to Sally. Sally buys a new bike for her son. The bike store owner deposits the $71.90 back into the bank. The bank loans $64.71 to Bill who spends it at the local bar.

That process continues until the bank has made $887 pure profit PLUS interest on John's original $100 deposit. Here are the numbers on each loan after Bill spends his currency at the bar. You really don't have to read them; I just want you to see how I arrived at $887.

The next loan is $58.24, then 52.41, 47.17, 42.45, 38.21, 34.39, 30.95, 27.85, 25.06, 22.56, 20.30, 18.27, 16.44, 14.80, 13.32, 11.99, 10.79, 9.71, 8.74, 7.86, 7.08, 6.37, 5.73, 5.16, 4.64, 4.18, 3.76, 3.38, 3.04, 2.74, 2.46, 2.22, 1.99, 1.79, 1.61, 1.45, 1.31, 1.18, 1.06, .95, .86, .77, .69, .62, .56, .50, .45, .40, .36, .33, .29, .26, .24, .21, .19, .17, .15, .14, .12, .11, .10, .09, .08, .07, .06, .06, .05, .05, .04, .04.

I give up. Just adding these together, you get $887. Just imagine, for every $100 deposited in any bank, the bank makes $887 profit BEFORE interest.

The compound interest on that amount of currency is way too much for my poor, little brain to tackle. It is important to note, the above example has been simplified. No bank loans such small amounts.

These amounts are part of much larger loans; however, the money still came from customer deposits and are recycled in the manner described.

Now, what I've described above is how the banking system worked back when they were on the Gold Standard. Back then, every dollar in the bank was supposed to be backed by a dollar's worth of gold.

As you can imagine, this bank-created new currency soon outnumbered the amount of gold value by 10 or more to one. The situation became so bad that President Richard Nixon had to take the WORLD off the Gold Standard in 1971 to keep the countries we owed money to from claiming all of the gold America had. America was and still is the main bank for the world.

In 1971, Nixon, with the stroke of a pen, converted the entire world to a FIAT money system. On that moment, the dollar "Certificate" became a dollar "Note". A Note by definition is an IOU; an IOU is by definition a debt. From that moment on, the world's money became debt-based and owed to the FED. The FED and all private banks now have the power to create UNLIMITED debt/currency OUT OF THIN AIR.

Chapter 10

Planned From the Beginning

Nixon did not know this was stage two of a two-part plan by the bankers the entire time. Part one happened in 1913; Nixon unwittingly delivered part two in 1971, the age of fiat. If the dollar was not tied to gold, then bankers were free to loan an unlimited amount of currency, as long as they kept a fraction of the deposits in the bank. Over time, as the need for cash was reduced by the use of credit and debit cards, that fraction kept getting smaller and smaller until banks now keep less than 0.1% of deposits.

I would guess, with fractional reserve lending, that would mean banks now make approximately $100,000 for every $100 deposit. That is still BEFORE interest.

♦ ♦ ♦

Since less and less people are using cash, banks no longer feel the need to keep more than 0.1% of cash on hand. Their two-part plan has just taken on a third part.

With no dollar-to-gold restraints and no need for physical cash, there is no limit to how much currency can be inflated.

Here is what that means for you. Every dollar that is deposited in the bank, over time, is multiplied thousands of times as new loans are granted.

When you borrow to buy a house or a car, the bank creates ALL of the currency applied to your account out of thin air. It is created digitally at the moment the loan is granted. This currency did not exist before this time, but you must pay hard-earned real currency to the bank as repayment. When you do, the entire amount is pure profit for the bank. Still, this is excluding interest.

As you make your monthly payments, each deposit is used to grant new loans, continuing the cycle of creating new currency that inflates the currency supply and devalues all dollars that existed before those new loans. As more currency enters the system, prices go up. This causes the cycle to start all over again, and again and again. Bankers knew, using the Rule of 72, there is no way to keep this currency — backed only by a government promise — working more than 50 years or so.

They devised a plan to run the value of currency down to nothing, indenturing the population to them in the process. Here's how that works: In the beginning, banks paid interest on your deposits to repay you for the use of your money.

Also, the interest paid helped your currency grow faster than inflation could rob it of its purchasing power. Now that they no longer have to adhere to the Gold Standard, and are creating new currency out of thin air, they no longer need your currency on deposit. No gold means no real money to protect.

The less cash they must keep on hand means the less they have to protect. Since all new currency is created by the bank, the bank no longer needs your currency to base new loans on.

So, now the banks have a right to charge you for keeping track of the currency they created, and you are not entitled to make as much, or any interest. Understand they are no longer using any money to back loans; they are creating new currency/money that solely belongs to them. Keeping track of and servicing your currency is now a SERVICE they can CHARGE YOU for.

Through the years banks have changed policies a number of times. The results have made sure that saving alone will not grow your currency above inflation. If inflation is 2% and the bank pays you 0.01%. Then your currency is losing 1.99% of purchasing power each year it sits in the bank. Plus, if you account for bank fees, it gets worse.

They have made the system punish you if you save. You must spend or lend currency in order to NOT lose value. Lower income people are hit the hardest. Let's say you have a savings account with less than $1,500 saved, and you are living paycheck to paycheck, so, what comes in goes out again each month.

If your account does not average $1500 over the entire month, the bank charges you $12 per month just to maintain your account. Let's see, 12x12=144. That is $144 per year that is being drained. If you average $1,000 or less each month, the percentage of your income taken goes up. So, if you are living hand to mouth or paycheck to paycheck as many people are, your money is being stolen at an alarming rate. I say stolen because, banks originally competed with one another for your business. Banks offered products, money, and prizes to entice people to bank with them.

All accounts were FREE no matter how much or little you had. In fact, they paid you in the form of interest just for having an account. They did this because it was your money they used as a foundation for new loans.

Now, because they create all currency out of thin air, your money is not needed. If you don't maintain over the minimum amount required, you must pay them to keep the account as they chip away at your value. No matter what, in today's banking, any fees you are charged will add up to more than the interest rate the bank is paying you.

Normal to low-income people will never grow their money in the bank. The system is set up to take what little value you have. This slow, sometimes rapid transfer of wealth moves value from you to the banks.

Eventually, when the dollar is worth nothing and we have a monetary reset, the debt owed to banks will be enormous. Who profits from this process? The OWNERS and high officers of the bank.

Chapter 11

Monetary Reset, New Money and

the War on Cash Begins

At some point the whole fiat monetary system must be reset. This must happen because as the value of currency heads toward zero, prices go up, causing more currency to be created. This process of reaching zero is called hyperinflation. At that point there is so much currency in circulation that it becomes easy to pay off the past debt if you are a government or large corporation.

However, at this time it might cost you and I over $5,000,000 to buy a loaf of bread. Think that can never happen? Ask the people of Venezuela, Argentina, Zimbabwe, and many other countries that have suffered through a monetary reset.

Once the currency of a country is recognized by all as being worth nothing, it must be replaced with something else of value. That something else of value coming from the banks will be a purely digital form of money.

This will remove all restraints from how much currency they can create and deliver directly to customer accounts.

Since the next version of money will NOT include cash, the banks transformation is almost complete. Banks started out as a safe place to store your money, meaning gold and silver. They have removed gold and silver as money, so now all that is left for them to protect is fiat cash. Currency backed by nothing more than a promise, is not new to the world. Every other attempt at a fiat system failed because physical cash existed.

If inflation caused you to need a truck load of cash to buy groceries, you'd figure there was something wrong with your currency. This has happened more times than I can count throughout history. This time, bankers had luck on their side in the form of advances in technology. Between the inventions of credit cards, debit cards and now digital cash – made possible by blockchain technology – banks have no further need for physical cash. It is now just as easy to carry a trillion dollars as it is to carry a single penny. They both take up the same amount of space and weigh the same. So, people might not complain if it costs $5,000,000 for a loaf of bread if they make $2 billion a month and have $5 trillion in their bank account.

Chapter 12

From Protectors to Creators

and Gatekeepers

Bankers, with the help of the government, have the population almost convinced that cash itself is dangerous. It's labeled as a tool of terrorists, drug pushers, money launderers, is unsanitary, and puts you in danger by carrying it.

Once people no longer feel a need for physical currency, or feel safer without it, the banks will be free to eliminate it altogether.

Make no mistake, banks control the government, not the other way around. Politicians will at some point propose the disillusion of cash.

Once cash is no longer used, the banks will have successfully transformed themselves from the protectors of money into the creators and gatekeepers of money.

Once all currency is digital and completely under their control, bankers effectively have complete control of the world.

Remember those famous words of Mr. Mayer Rothschild, founder of the Rothschild banking dynasty, **"Give me control of a nation's money supply and I care not who makes its laws."**

Allowing digital currency to be under the control of bankers is like putting a bear in charge of guarding a stack of honey pots. Have you heard the phrase, "Asking the fox to guard the hen house?"

They would create as much digital cash as they need. There would never be another bank run because the banks could pump digital currency into every consumer's account whenever they needed to.

If a country was undergoing a financial crisis, the bank could just inject currency into every person's account directly to ease the economy through. That sounds great except everyone would be in more debt at the end. Inflation would again eat away at your purchasing power. The value of currency saved would be diminished.

On the flip side, the banks AND the government would have the ability to turn anyone's access to currency on and off like a light.

Not to mention the ability to monitor every penny you get and spend. Once the U.S. dollar is completely digital, the bank, through normal inflation combined with massive quantitative easing (QE) to protect the world from entering deep depressions, will reach its ultimate goal, control of the world through its finances. At some point in the near future, the U.S. dollar will inflate itself to worthlessness.

The world bank, using the International Monetary Fund will issue its own digital currency based on the Special Drawing Rights (SDR) unit of value they created. All monies of the world will be valued against the SDR. The USA will be no more important than any other country at that point. Banks created the problem, delivered the cure, and will take full control.

To recap: Banks started out keeping our money safe. They ultimately replaced money with currency that only they could issue. Then they removed that which gave the currency its value (gold/silver). With nothing to limit them, they printed paper currency until it has little to no value.

Now they want to eliminate printed currency so they can simply push a few keys on a computer to create an unlimited amount of digital currency at will.

Hey, I want that job. I get to create something from nothing. I am the only one who can do this. Everyone in the WORLD must use what I create, by force of law, and no one in the world has legal jurisdiction over me.

After I loan currency out, I must be paid back more currency, through interest, than I have created. So, everyone must come back to me to create more in order to pay me back what they owe now. That means they'll owe me even more later. Plus, since it is digital currency, every time currency changes hands it must go through me so I can take a cut (transaction fees). Then I get to do this forever. Oh yeah, I want that job!

♦ ♦ ♦

I can see a day when other stores of value will fall under the attack of banks. Things like individual property being mortgaged and foreclosed on to the point that the banks and big business (owned by banks) own everything, and most regular people own nothing.

Why bother or burden yourself with the worries of ownership? Wouldn't it be easier to rent everything? That way, you can always have the latest gadget, or move whenever you like.

Why buy a car, home, computer, program, appliances, or any other thing and have to worry about upkeep, maintenance, and disposal of when done. Just rent everything. What would you call people in a world where most individuals own nothing? What could make that world possible?

Chapter 13

Government And Bank Closed Digital Currency

As I write this, the next level of control is being perfected. China is experimenting with Social Credit Scores. Most countries have a credit score that is tied to how well we pay our bills and how well we repay loans granted to us. If we are late on rent, utilities, car notes and the like, our credit score goes down. With a low score, when we apply for any loan or try to rent anything, our cost for that loan will be much higher than someone with a better credit score.

In China, over 99% of the people use digital money. This money is passed from the bank to the merchant or vendor through a phone apps like WeChat Pay or Alipay.

These apps allow the Chinese people to do things like purchase goods and services, make reservations, tip waiters, send money to friends, and pay their rent and bills. No one uses cash any longer.

In fact, most places will not accept cash. Having all currency in digital form allows the government to completely track every cent people earn and spend.

It also allows the government to grade you as a citizen. Based on what and where you buy, give to charity, and donate politically, your score is calculated. Buy cigarettes, too many drugs (legal or otherwise), too much alcohol, insult or say the wrong thing about someone high in power, jaywalk or litter—your score goes down. If your score is too low, you are placed on a restricted list. If you have friends or relatives on the restricted list, YOUR score goes down. With a high score you are free to go and come as you please and are granted many perks and privileges those with low scores don't have.

Once on this restricted list, you can lose your job, or have no access to trains, airports, or even Uber. Travel outside of your local area is forbidden. You are forced to continue to live in your current place because no one else can legally rent to you. No matter how much currency you have, where you can spend it is very limited. The point of mentioning China is the control governments can exhort on individual citizens when it can access on what and where you spend your currency.

Governments or even banks can determine when your currency is good or not. Government controlled digital currency gives too much control of your life to those in power. You might be saying to yourself, "That's China. This could never happen here in America."

Well, answer this question: Why are airports, bus, and train stations here in America installing the very same facial recognition video systems China uses? Under the guise of keeping America safe, widespread dispersion of high-resolution video surveillance with facial recognition abilities are being planned and installed across this nation.

As China proves and refines the concept, America will slowly integrate the very same policies under the banner of public safety and encouraging good citizenship. Britain has had cameras everywhere for years. Their citizens are getting used to and coming to rely on their CCTV system for many things. The right PR spin from the government could motivate the majority of U.S. citizens to outright demand we follow China's lead.

With these systems in place, think of how much easier it would be for police to find the bad guys. With these systems, they might stop crime before it happens.

People might feel safe walking down the street knowing their every step is being recorded in case someone assaults them. If they are the victim of an accident, public video could prove their case. Great, but it also gives the government the ability to collect data on what you do, where you go, what you buy, who you travel with and who you just happen to be near, whether you know them or not. In China, every chance encounter is caught on video. You will stay on the restricted list, until you prove you don't really know that person you were recorded talking to.

People, please realize, **it is impossible to be completely safe without being completely under someone's observation and control.** Remember another famous quote, **"Those who give up a little freedom for the sake of safety, will ultimately find that they are neither free nor safe."**

All the tools needed for George Orwell's "1984" to come to pass are in existence now. The only difference is, in our modern version, computers, not people will be watching and taking notes. Now let me bring this back to the subject of money. Private bank or government digital currency is the key to making the conglomerate of bankers' and governments' plans come true.

Without digital currency, they can watch us but not control us. As long as we, the people, have a method of earning and spending money without the eyes and/or permission of the government or banks, we will forestall total domination.

Chapter 14

Open Digital Money - Cryptocurrencies

Cryptocurrencies that are self-issued and self-controlled are called Open. While the records kept on a closed digital currency are only accessible by their controllers, and those records can be manipulated by those same controllers, open digital money can be monitored by any and everyone. However, open cryptocurrencies cannot be controlled or manipulated by anyone, not even those who built it. Open digital money can be adjusted somewhat by those in charge of processing the network, but most aspects of an open currency cannot be changed by anyone.

Bitcoin, for example, can never be inflated beyond the 21,000,000 limit hard coded in the system. However, the world community that supports the network can vote to change the behavior of the coin.

For example: Right now, bitcoin is divisible to the 8th decimal place. That means there are one hundred million pieces in each bitcoin.

The community could vote to make it divisible to the 16th decimal place. Which would mean each bitcoin would contain one hundred QUADRILLION pieces. That won't change the value of bitcoin, just allow it to be bought, sold, and spent in smaller pieces, like changing a dollar into pennies or pennies into one-tenth of pennies.

With open cryptocurrencies, no one can ever be stopped from spending their money anywhere that accepts it. But this too will enable the government to track your income and spending habits. Those concerned about privacy will want to, at times, use privacy-centered cryptocurrencies.

Cryptocurrencies centered on privacy will allow anyone to see what was spent but not who spent or received it. Governments fear this type of cryptocurrency most. Without the ability to track money, the government loses its largest weapon.

Chapter 15

Money as A Weapon

In 1971, the US government decided to enlist banks in their war on crime, so the Bank Secrecy Act was signed into law. This act forced banks to become an extended arm of the government. It required banks to spy on and report financial activities of their customers.

That act was modified over the years to require banks to know many private things about every person and/or organization connected to any account. The bank must know who they are, where they were born, what they do for money, what their lifestyle is like, and much, much more.

It also requires the bank to report any change in banking habits and activities. Should your business struggle for a while then suddenly start doing well; the bank has to report that to the government. If you make or sell anything and deposit a larger than normal amount of cash, they must know where the currency came from.

If you take too much currency out of the bank at once, they MUST file a Suspicious Activity Report (SAR) and they are forbidden by law to let you know they are filing the report.

Each time you withdraw over a certain amount, a new SAR is filed. Should you want or need to withdraw a large amount of cash, the bank must ask WHY you need it. If your explanation is not good enough for them, you may not get the currency and a report will be filed.

If you write a large check or need to wire any amount of money, the recipient will automatically be checked against a list of people, organizations, and countries Americans are forbidden to do business with.

If they are on the list, no currency will be transmitted, and a SAR will be filed against you. When there was only physical cash, governments had to fight crime the old-fashioned way — they had to work.

Once digital currency outnumbered physical currency, they discovered it was easier to track and control the currency than to do detective work. Now that currency has become mostly digital, governments find it easy to force banks to freeze a depositor's account.

In fact, it is just as easy to freeze the accounts of an entire country as it is to block a person. Thus, money has become a weapon. As long as you must ask permission to access or spend your own currency, that currency does NOT belong to you.

Chapter 16

Whose Currency Is It?

Most people have no idea they have signed away their rights to the currency they deposit into any bank. That currency instantly becomes the sole property of the bank the moment you let it go. They have the right to keep it, spend it, loan it, and lose it. You have no legal recourse to regain what was yours under certain circumstances.

Case in point: The bank gets robbed, electronically. They lose $50,000,000. You had $800,000 deposited. The insurance on the accounts belongs to the bank not you. When the insurance is paid, the bank is obligated to replace only $250,000 in your account. That is a net loss to you of $550,000 you will never see again. In order to not suffer this loss, you must open four bank accounts and never have more than $250K in any one. Likewise, if the government is too deep in debt, they have the right to say to every bank in America, "Take X% out of all your depositor's accounts and give it to us to repay our debts."

Think I'm kidding? Try reading the fine print in your bank account contract, or, better yet, ask anyone from Greece. It happened to them after the 2009 banking crisis. If someone can refuse to give you what you consider yours, then you were mistaken in thinking it belonged to you.

Chapter 17

We're All One Big Happy Family

You ask, "Why do I keep bringing up these other countries?" It is because almost every country operates under the same banking system. They all follow — for the most part — the same policies and rules. Every bank whose currency is backed by the U.S. dollar, operates under the banking rules of the International Monetary Fund.

For the most part, all customer contracts are written with the same provisions. What happens in one country can happen in every country.

Think of the banks of the world as being under one corporate head. Just like Hilton Hotels owns Waldorf Astoria Hotels & Resorts, Conrad Hotels & Resorts, Canopy, DoubleTree, Embassy Suites Hotels, Hampton Hotels, Homewood Suites, Home Suites and Grand Vacations, the IMF owns or controls every central bank in the world whose currency interacts with or is backed by the U.S. dollar.

While the above-mentioned hotel chains may seem to be competitors to the average person, they, in fact, send their profits to the same head company. That company dictates how each branch chain will operate. Once you understand the banks of the world are owned or controlled by one huge organization, you might be open to accepting that ONE family owns or controls them all.

Originally the banking family of Rothschild controlled the banks of Europe. The patriarch's five sons were each sent to London, Paris, Frankfurt, Vienna, and Naples to start banking businesses.

As I write this, the Rothschild family controls banking in all but THREE countries. In 2003, only Afghanistan, Iraq, Sudan, Libya, Cuba, North Korea, and Iran did not have Rothschild controlled central banks. From 2011 to today, only Cuba, North Korea, and Iran remain without a Rothschild central bank.

Do you notice these are all countries the U.S. has had major disagreements with or been at war with over the past seventy years? Think for a moment: the money in every country in the WORLD is under the control of a Rothschild central bank except the countries the U.S. is in conflict with.

Once the Rothschilds establish a banking relationship with any country, they suddenly stop being an enemy of the USA. China is the exception. Even though they have a Rothschild central bank, there is such a thing as playing for both sides.

China is working hard to replace the USA as the world's leading financial power. Our dollar is the reserve currency of the world because the Rothschild family controls the United States Federal Reserve Bank. For the few of you who do not know it yet, the FED is a PRIVATE, for-profit corporation owned by the Rothschild family conglomerate.

Chapter 18

The Future Fight for Control

Imagine you are the family that controls the world through its money. Now something comes along that gives everyone under your control the ability to replace you. Think how — with all the power, control, and influence you command — how hard you will fight to maintain dominance and control.

You have the financial strings of every news, TV, and radio outlet, along with the most powerful and influential political figures and celebrities at your command.

You can influence entire governments. You have the ability to shape public opinion by disgracing or jailing any celebrity that dares support your rival. If you control money and want to continue, there is no stone you can't or won't turn in order to make sure this power usurper is put and kept in its place. For 10 years the public around the world were told how Bitcoin was nothing — a scam, a bubble, a game of the bigger fool, super risky, a fraud.

Yet after 10 years of trying to squash this little bug, Bitcoin has emerged as the most profitable investment in the history of investing. People around the world are discovering the abilities and benefits of cryptocurrencies.

The financial world is changing day by day, faster than anyone has ever seen it change. All because of the invention of the blockchain that is Bitcoin. Over the next 5 to 10 years, as the heat is turned up, we, the public, will find ourselves the pawns in this war for financial control. I'm sure there will be many laws passed with the aim of curtailing the expansion of open cryptocurrencies.

Even more laws will be written to squash privacy-centered cryptocurrencies. Most of these laws will be given to us to "protect" us from money launderers, terrorists, pedophiles, and drug dealers.

Under the guise of protecting us from ourselves, the powers that be will do all in their power to make the lives of anyone who dares to challenge the right of the central bank to control money a living hell. Don't be fooled; the real motive for these laws will be for governments to maintain a tax base, and for the banks to keep us under a debt-based, inflationary monetary system.

In the long run, the will of the people shall triumph. People in places where banks do not exist, are and will be using free, open, border-less, censorship resistant, immutable money that is controlled by nothing but mathematics. Mathematics cannot be corrupted or changed to force favor on one group over another.

Since the closed digital currency, the central banks want us to use also needs the internet to work, I think they will have a hard time stopping people from using internet money that controls itself and becomes more valuable the longer you have it.

Chapter 19

Governments, Banks, Taxes, and the

Enslavement of Our Unborn

No one questions the government's right to tax the public. No one questions that taxes are needed to fund the activities of the government. Almost everyone feels it is right for everyone to pay their fair share of taxes.

Here's the problem: Everyone should question the activities of the government that steer wealth from the masses to a very few. Everyone should question policies that are devised to enslave our children and our children's children. Let's look at how our government is funded. For the moment, let us pretend there is zero dollars in existence.

Our government has just been formed. To finance the activities needed to run the government, Congress creates a single bank. The bank has no money in it because none exists yet. Congress gives the bank the sole responsibility to CREATE money and LOAN it to the government.

The government tells all of its people this new money will be good for all debt, public and private. The government creates an income tax for the public, so it can repay the loan to the bank. The government determines it will need $2 million the first year and $80,000 per year to operate. The first act of this bank is to create — out of thin air — $2 million, which it lends to the government at a 3% annual interest rate.

Now the government spends the $2 million by purchasing needed goods and services from the public. This creates an economy. As people pay their income taxes, which are set at 10%, the government collects 10% of $2 million, which is $200,000. They pay 3% interest on $2 million ($60,000) to the bank and another $60,000 on the principal, then use the balance of $80,000 to run the government for the next year.

Can you see the two grave errors in this? If the government borrowed $2 million and owes $2 million plus 3% a year, where is the extra 3% a year going to come from? There is ONLY 2 two million dollars in existence!

No matter what happens, at some point, the government OR someone else is going to have to borrow more money from the bank in order to fully repay the original loan.

Eventually, you can pay the entire amount of the loan just in interest and still owe on the loan principal. At that point you must borrow more money, and the extra money borrowed gets added to the debt, plus new interest.

As long as interest is created while not being part of the loan, mathematically, there is NO WAY TO EVER REPAY what was borrowed. I'll repeat that. There is no way to repay MORE money than there is in existence. Thus, you must continue to borrow MORE which prompts the bank to create more.

The second problem with this picture is, the $120,000 paid to the bank is money that is out of circulation and in the hands of the bank owners until such time as they see fit to spend it into the economy. The bank made $120,000 profit in one year from creating something from nothing.

Watered down and way over simplified, this is exactly how almost every government in the world is funded. The bankers' profit is at least 3% of the balance owed each year. If the debt were stable, which it cannot be, that would mean the bank would profit 3% each year of the $2 million loan.

At some point, the bank would have earned back most of the original $2 million just in interest. So, how does the government ever repay the loan without continuing to borrow more and more money?

The answer is THEY NEVER CAN. You will NEVER see the government vote NOT to extend the National Debt. Every time it comes up for a vote, it will pass. If they don't, the nation will have to declare bankruptcy and the bankers will take possession of the nation.

Please do the math. This system we find ourselves under is just a giant borrowing Ponzi scheme. The bank says we will loan you all the money you want, but the meaning hidden in the fine print says when you stop borrowing, we will own everything you have.

This unholy arrangement will continue until our great grand-children's grandchildren are born owing millions of dollars. Without the amount of currency in existence being limited by or tied to some finite commodity, there is no limit as to how much debt can be created.

So, no matter how much currency is created or how long this continues, there will NEVER be enough currency in existence to fully repay the ever-growing DEBT.

The above scenario is the exact reason our founding fathers fought against ever forming a central bank. In fact, the current incarnation of the FED is the third central bank this country has had. Unfortunately, this time, they may be too large and powerful to undo.

CHAPTER 20

Debt Is the Problem

The one constant in everything I've explained to you is, the bank creates currency, then lends that currency to the government or you with interest. There is a little-known fact banks would move heaven and earth to make us forget: The U.S. Constitution gives Congress the right to CREATE money. Yes, I said to create, not borrow.

Congress could decide to end the FED and simply create enough money to run our economy and maybe even the world economies. We have done it successfully before for short periods of time. Each time we did, the central banks plotted, bribed, and murdered to reestablish control. Again, little known facts: America, under President Andrew Jackson, dissolved the central bank, paid off our debts and was very successful in growing the U.S. economy between 1833 and 1837. Jackson was and still is the only president to completely pay the American debt down to zero. The first American president to ever have his life threatened was also Jackson.

In the middle of his fight with the bank, a man approached him and fired TWO guns at his stomach. Fortunately, both misfired. Part of the would-be assassin's reasoning was, with Jackson dead, money would be more plentiful.

In order to regain monetary control of the country, the regional banks created a depression and blamed both Jackson and Congress' control of money for it. It took years of manipulation, bribery, and propaganda for the banks to convince the American people that money would be better controlled by financial professionals than politicians. Abraham Lincoln also successfully moved the U.S. government away from central bank control. He created money without debt, fiat currency of his day.

This action was so successful and threatening to the banks that they publicly declared the U.S. be destroyed or it would take over the world. Instead of destroying the country, they killed Lincoln and destroyed his money system before it could destroy them.

Here is a reprint from the 1865 London Times: **"If this mischievous financial policy, which has its origin in North America, shall become indurated down to a fixture, then that Government will furnish its own money without cost.**

It will pay off debts and be without debt. It will have all the money necessary to carry on its commerce. It will become prosperous without precedent in the history of the world. The brains, and wealth of all countries will go to North America. That country must be destroyed or it will destroy every monarchy on the globe."

Some say this article was never written. You have the advantage of looking back on history. You decide if it is true or not. Please note, Lincoln was assassinated in this same year. Then, the banks had Lincoln's greenbacks tied to gold and silver, the central bank was rechartered, and we see who owns most of the world today. Here are more facts that banks would rather you never know.

As I mentioned earlier, the FED is the THIRD incarnation of the American Central Bank. Each of the two prior attempts drove this country to the brink of financial ruin. Each major depression and recession has been the result of central and regional bank actions. Either the banks caused the depressions or recessions to persuade the people that we needed them (1839–1907), or they caused the financial unrest through their inept handling of the economy (1929-1933). There have been over 40 recessions or depressions in the U.S.

Every boon or bust period has served to either make banks rich through uncontrolled lending or to make banks rich through transfers of wealth brought about by foreclosures. In every case, banks profited from both the success and failure of our economy. In 1891, the American Bankers Association, wrote the following to its member banks: **"On September 1st, 1894, we will not renew our loans under any consideration. On September 1st we will demand our money. We will foreclose and become mortgagees in possession. We can take two-thirds of the farms west of the Mississippi, and thousands of them east of the Mississippi as well, at our own price... Then the farmers will become tenants as in England."**

This was printed in the U.S. Congressional Record on April 29, 1913. Just in case you didn't notice the dates involved here, this was published to the member banks THREE YEARS in advance. Banks are NOT your friend. Today, instead of planning mass foreclosures, banks entice us, with low rates, to refinance every time we build equity in our property. They say, "Don't let that money just sit there." We are encouraged to lease cars instead of buying them. "Get a NEW car every three years."

Each time we refinance, we extend the time we are indebted. Until we hold the deed, we OWN NOTHING and are the same as tenants.

Chapter 21

My Opinion

This seems like a good place to inject a comment or two. Because the U.S. dollar is the reserve currency for the world, America can issue its own fiat digital currency with no debt attached, then use interest on loans to other countries along with income and sales tax to recycle money to the government — then limit the creation of new currency to the direst of circumstances. The process of creating new currency must be almost as difficult as adding an amendment to the constitution.

And/Or, we should put NON-banking academics in charge of developing and implementing monetary policy and pay them well for life. We should outlaw lobbying these people and make sure no one in the process has any possibility to profit, from, before, or after decisions or policies are made.

There should be very heavy retroactive penalties on them and any person(s), business(es) or for-profit group(s) they are later discovered to have acted on behalf of.

Finally, we should tie future, after-service bonuses to policies and programs that prove over time to benefit or protect the economy. In short, take all outside profit out of the creation and administration of economic policies/money and reward those responsible for policies that prove over time to work.

To control inflation, make sure new currency created through fractional reserve lending (should that practice still be allowed) is strictly limited to 90% of money wholly owned by the lending institution. Make banks custodians of customer deposits, not owners of customer deposits. This is great, because until the banks earn it, they can't lend it, and they will be limited to lending only ninety cents for each dollar they own. If the lending of customer deposits is permitted, MAKE SURE the interest paid to those depositors and savers is at least 3% above REAL inflation by law.

Every reason economists claim creating currency without debt is bad, is exactly what is happening under our present debt-based system. The only difference is under our current system, our ever-enlarging debt is owed to bankers; while if we just created currency without debt, the only drawback would be the possibility of inflation. Well, we have inflation now with piles of debt on top of it.

Chapter 22

Time to Think Outside the Box

We are used to thinking in terms of earning MORE, making more, and investing more, when we should be thinking about creating the POWER to purchase more. Purchasing more, called purchasing power, is what is important. It should not matter if we pay less or make less, as long as when we go to buy something, the money we earned in yesteryear buys more this year than it did then.

What is the purpose of saving and investing if not to be able to buy as much, if not more, tomorrow than you can buy today? It makes no sense to save money for years if that money cannot purchase at least as much as it could the day it was saved.

We live in a world where you can grow the number of dollars in your possession and still be able to purchase less than when you started saving or investing. Think back to the house story at the beginning of this book.

The house originally sold in 1970 for 754 ounces of gold, both worth $26,400. In 2019 the house is worth $585,000 which is only 433 ounces of gold. That represents a LOSS of 321 ounces of gold worth $433,350. The investment gained massively in dollars but lost $433 thousand dollars in purchasing power/value. Because of bank-driven inflation, the purchasing power of the dollar is shrinking faster than its numbers are growing in our accounts.

I personally believe a deflationary economy would be best for everyone in the long run. A deflationary economy would see purchasing power increase over time, reward people for saving, and see prices and wages reduced over time. This would allow the purchasing power of money to grow. This would mean interest is not needed for the value (purchasing power) of savings or loaned money to increase.

In that economy, controlling the rate of deflation becomes as important as controlling the rate of inflation is now. The major difference is, with deflation the people prosper. With inflation the banks prosper. After thousands of years of a "more is better attitude," I know a true deflationary economy will not happen in my lifetime, but the concept is sound.

Capitalism and a deflationary economy can coexist just as easily as our current arrangement. Those who are in charge of creating money and charging interest for doing so, have and will work hard to convince the world that a deflationary economy would be the worst thing imaginable.

That is because they know a deflationary economy will create a world in which they must work just as hard as the rest of us to make an honest day's living. Their efforts will always be to make sure such a world shall never exist. The major argument against a deflationary economy is that it would make borrowed money harder to repay as time goes on.

If people are earning less because money is worth more over time, then money paid back at the end of the loan would be worth more than money paid at the beginning of the loan. They are right.

That is why only people who need money for growing their income or people who need money for a real emergency would ever consider borrowing. In our present debt-based, inflationary economy, if people stopped going into debt, the economy would collapse into nothingness.

You really need to understand that the process of BORROWING money is the only thing keeping the world economy alive today.

In a deflationary world, if prices are getting lower over time and money buys more over time, the process of saving becomes more valuable.

This is another reason that economists use to declare deflation as a bad thing. The rationale is that people will not spend as much today because prices will come down later.

Think. There are over seven billion people on this planet. Providing them with food, clothing, shelter, fun, entertainment, travel, and all the other little things necessary to make life worth living should be enough to keep any economy going, growing, and thriving.

Anyone who thinks people are going to put off feeding themselves, going on vacation, or purchasing materials to grow their business just because it might be a little cheaper a year from now, is in my opinion, crazy.

Bankers want you to believe that if currency is not continuously moving, the economy will suffer.

Bottom line: The financial system is broken. It is keeping us all broke. It is a rigged game MOST CANNOT win. Through growing debt and increasing taxes, we will see our children's children born in debt and subject to financial slavery.

Once we start using the NEW bank issued digital money after the financial RESET, we will have NO financial privacy and even less financial security. We have never had the tools, the ability, and most importantly the power to fix this mess until now.

Learn what these tools are and how to use them. One example of something we should learn is what makes Bitcoin better than Gold.

Chapter 23

How Bitcoin is Better Gold

Than Gold

The characteristics of money are portable, recognizable, durable, divisible, and scarce. Gold has all of these. That is why it has been used as money for over 5,000 years. Let's look at each and compare gold to bitcoin.

Divisible: You can divide gold into smaller and smaller pieces. However, after you get down to a certain size, the pieces become harder and harder to keep track of. A single bitcoin on the other hand, can be divided into many trillions of parts and each part is as secure and trackable as the whole.

Scarce: Gold is being found everyday. As gold becomes more valuable, more is being located and mined. There is talk of mining asteroids and other planets in the future. One day, technology may advance to the point that gold may be produced in a laboratory. Many factors can and do influence the total amount of gold in existence.

The total amount of bitcoin is known and can NEVER be increased. As long as the Bitcoin network exists, that amount of bitcoin will exist. There is nothing anyone can or will ever be able to do to increase the maximum amount of bitcoin. It is an absolute finite amount and there is only ONE source. So, by definition, it is scarce.

Portable: This is the weakest feature of gold. While it is easy to carry around in small amounts, the more you have, the heavier and bulkier it becomes. Having gold on your person or in your home could put you and your loved ones in danger. Gold must be protected, secured, and verified, which costs you money. You can carry a trillion dollars' worth of bitcoin in the same space and with the same effort it takes to carry one penny. Unless you tell someone where to look, no one can find it or steal it, even if they do find it.

Recognizable: Everyone knows what gold looks like. However, you need some sort of verifying process to be sure of the weight and quality of your gold. Then there are those who have been fooled by gold-covered lead. The Bitcoin network validates and verifies each bitcoin, or part thereof, at each transaction. Bitcoin CANNOT be counterfeited or debased in any way.

Durability: Here gold has a leg up on Bitcoin. Gold is impossible to destroy. When mankind and the Earth are gone, gold will still exist. Bitcoin will cease to exist the moment the last computer with a record of the blockchain is destroyed.

Chapter 24

Bitcoin over Gold, Until...

Bitcoin shall serve as a store of value; bitcoin is what gold and other more functional cryptocurrencies will use as a base. It is just as the U.S. dollar is the current base instrument for most world currencies.

Bitcoin will serve the function gold once did as a financial base. The great thing about this will be that NO ONE NEEDS TO PROTECT, VERIFY, OR VALIDATE IT. There will be no need for a Fort Knox, a bank, or any other monetary safe place; the Bitcoin blockchain performs all those functions itself. Even though bitcoin will become the true and ultimate reserve monetary base, it is my opinion that gold and bitcoin will work together to secure the world's finances. It makes no difference to me if bitcoin is denoted in gold or if gold is denoted in bitcoin. They both will survive as a means to hold or transfer value. I give bitcoin the edge only because there is a KNOWN FINITE amount of bitcoin and gold, though rare, will never be finite.

I can see a day when people exchange their gold for bitcoin in order to purchase a house or car. Or in the case of someone needing to flee a hostile area, exchange their gold for bitcoin in order to take their wealth with them without danger.

Passing an inheritance via a crypto wallet is easier and faster than having a bank transfer ownership. I can think of at least 10 other reasons – to change gold into bitcoin. Unfortunately, I can only think of one reason to change Bitcoin into gold. That being, should something happen to the electrical grid, or the internet, Bitcoin will be USELESS. It will still exist, but you'll have no way to access it.

Gold has proven its value; its physical nature is both a curse and a blessing. We are in the very beginning of the transition from using horses as our main way of transportation to a world dominated by the car. Bitcoin is the car; gold is the horse. Just like horses are still around and valuable, until something happens to render cars useless, cars will dominate. If cars are ever rendered useless, those with horses will be in the driver's seat. No one says you can't own both. In the meantime, each one can play its part to support the world.

Chapter 25

The Solution

Capitalism is a great thing. It can work quite well for those who follow sound money principals. Savers can protect their future by putting their savings into sound money and NOT currency. The following steps will assure you grow and prosper no matter where on the financial ladder you start out.

Note: For a variety of reasons NOTHING on this list is easy to accomplish. If it were, there would be less people in poverty and economic slavery.

1. NEVER borrow unless it is an emergency, or you are borrowing in order to make money. That includes never using credit cards except when the purchase will quickly earn more money than you are paying.

2. Save currency ONLY for short-term (less than a year) goals. As long as we are in an inflationary, debt-based economy, inflation makes the long-term saving of currency stupid.

3. Never save long-term using any currency. Save for long-term goals by purchasing only stores of value items: like gold, silver, cryptocurrencies, and land/property. Stocks and bonds are NOT stores of value.

Do your own research to determine which items are the best stores of value. You have the ultimate responsibility to grow and protect your value. The important thing is that you CHANGE your currency into something that is NOT dollars or based on the value of a dollar.

You want something that is valued in dollars but not whose value is determined by the value of dollars. Example: Land, gold, and cryptocurrencies can be purchased with dollars. However, you can trade them for other things without using dollars at all.

If the dollar disappeared over night, these things would still maintain value and could be traded for goods and services. The value they maintain is what you want to possess.

Whatever form the new money takes, the value of these things will remain the same, and that is how you protect your purchasing power.

4. Save for long-term EVERY WEEK. Whether it is one dollar or one thousand dollars, put some amount into real stores of value EVERY paycheck. Take part of your value and put it OUTSIDE the system. This is how you PAY yourself FIRST. As true stores of value increase in purchasing power over time, a very small amount saved today can grow into a huge amount of value in the years to come.

5. Purchase only what you need. Spending funds on the latest gadget, fashions, designer labels, new cars, fast foods, junk foods, and the like will ensure you stay financially enslaved.

6. Purchase only with cash, cryptocurrencies, or debit cards. If you don't have the money, you can't afford it at this time.

7. If you must use a credit card, make sure you only use less than one-fourth of your available balance AND make sure you pay the entire amount back within 30 to 90 days.

8. Unless you have enough stored up to live without income for a MINIMUM of one year, you do not need to buy anything on credit. No cars, clothes, high priced restaurants, electronics, or luxury items of any kind.

The EXCEPTION to this rule is if any or all of these items are needed for you to make money. If the item will put more income into your pocket than it took out, it works. Once you purchase, see rule #7.

9. Remember, every dollar you spend on something you don't actually NEED, translates into hundreds of future LOST dollars in real money, savings, and investments.

10. Remember banks are NOT your friends. Their job is to motivate you to borrow currency, spend as much as you take in, and deposit as much as you get, so they can earn profit. They make profit every time you move currency in and out of the bank.

The longer your funds are in the bank, the more value/purchasing power you lose by default. The old saying, "A penny saved is a penny earned," has been flipped on its head. It is still true, but now it is the bank that earns the penny.

11. Having said all that about banks and credit cards, if you take the time to learn how to be your own bank, you can use processes like Velocity Banking and Infinite Banking to play the bank's game and win big time.

VB and IB are simple and effective methods of using the bank's money to get out of debt and multiply your net worth. They both require time, learning and self-discipline. For an explanation of VB and IB, look them up. They both tie into Rule #1, using credit to make money instead of spending money.

12. Bitcoin is not the only cryptocurrency you should learn about. There are others that serve functions other than money. All of the ones that will be around in 10 years shall be worth thousands of times more than they are today. Learn about them and determine which ones you think will stand the test of time. The money you put into a cup of coffee today could buy you a car in 10 to 20 years. That is, if we are still buying cars.

Conclusion

Most of us were ignorant before we read this book. Our actions were those of someone without knowledge. We blindly did what we were told by those in authority. It was not our fault.

Do your own research and confirm the writings within these pages. If, after you confirm what I've told you and still solely rely on a monetary system intentionally designed to financially enslave you, then go back to the glossary at the start of this book to see the "S", "F", and "I" words your future actions will fall under. Unlike before you read this book, you now have a choice. Our present system isn't going anywhere anytime soon. Our physical fiat cash will be replaced by a purely digital cash, but it will be the same old worthless currency with the same faults and more flaws. Until changes are made, I suggest everyone slowly start to implement the rules I've outlined. Start moving a part of your net worth out of this debt-based, inflationary lake of quicksand.

We are under the thumb of the most powerful people the world has ever seen. They will not go quietly into the night. Their financial power and human puppets in government will make sure anyone who believes in human financial liberty is cast as a communist, socialist, criminal, uneducated imbecile, and should be jailed or worse.

They are trying to protect what they have. Wouldn't you do the same? It is up to the majority of us to learn about and take advantage of the new tools we have access to. It is time to look at this position/situation all those well-educated, rich, and powerful people have led us to suffer through. We, the masses, earn $1 for every $10,000 they earn. We respect them for being able to earn that much and we strive to do the same. Very few ever do and that is the problem. I think it is time to consider moving to a monetary system that is outside the control of those who benefit the greatest from controlling it.

There will always be those who have more than others; that's capitalism. However, capitalism was never meant to create the one percent that controls more wealth than the other ninety nine percent combined. That was accomplished through dishonesty and greed.

Throughout history, greed has pushed mankind into wars, and to do unthinkably horrible things to people we don't know. Those with financial power in the pursuit of even more wealth have caused pain, suffering, and death to millions — most of it financed by bankers. It does not matter whether the aggressors were individuals, dictators, or elected governments — they all were financed by bankers. Bankers could not fulfill this function if they were not in charge of creating currency.

If currency were created based on the number of people it is meant to serve, and the currency supply was safely stored by the people themselves, it would be up to the people to support government aggression.

This has never been possible before. Earlier I mentioned, people don't want to waste time thinking about something they have no power to change. For the first time in history, we NOW have the tools to construct and enlist a system of monetary control that is independent, fair, and stable.

There is no reason, IF an inflationary system is to be continued, that it cannot be made to run and automatically adjust itself to maintain a stable economy based on the size of the population it serves.

Fiat-loaned into existence or increased irresponsibly has been the root cause of thousands of fiat currency failures. Remember, throughout history there has NEVER been a fiat currency that has NOT failed. That failure has ALWAYS been because the currency supply has been increased or decreased by people who profit from that control. Money should be sound/stable. Currency should represent and be based on sound money. If that is the case, then in my humble opinion, a deflationary economy would serve the public best in the long run.

Aside from people overcoming the great difficulty of accepting less pay without being insulted—Deflation stores value in and for those who can save. Especially if you don't need to pay someone to keep your money safe. Inflation only benefits those who create new currency at interest, and then profit from each transfer of currency from one hand to another.

The creation, maintenance, control, and distribution of money should NOT be in the hands of those who profit directly from those actions, be they governments, institutions, or individuals. It might be time for mankind to step aside and let mathematics control the supply of money to society.

I can see a world that uses one monetary standard, as long as no single nation or group of nations, state or authority is in control of its administration. There could be a different currency issued for every country (though I don't recommend that), that is all tied or based on that one standard. Blockchain and cryptocurrencies may be the answer. But that is a subject for another time.

Epilogue

I have not tried to give you a complete accounting of money and its history. There are literally hundreds of other authors who have written wonderfully expansive books, movies, and documentaries on the subject.

I have done my best to keep this book short and simple. I care about how we and our children must live with and through the consequences of actions and implemented laws that were forced upon us as a result of events in history. This is where we are. How can we best protect ourselves and move forward?

People who have fared the best financially, both in and out of the banking world, have been those who moved a good portion of their value outside the dollar-based system. These people buy things that are valued IN dollars not ON dollars. It is my belief that doing so is the best way to protect and grow your wealth. Cryptocurrencies are a new tool rich and poor people have equal access to. They are so new that $10 worth of the right coin or token can be worth millions of dollars in the future.

The first purchase with bitcoin was paying 10,000 bitcoin for two pizzas. At this writing, bitcoin's price is $10,371 per coin. The person who sold the pizzas collected $103,710,000. Bitcoin was only the first to do this. I don't think it will be the last. There are thousands of cryptos and in time, there will be thousands more. Most are scams, cons, and outright junk. Don't let others tell you what to put your money in or on. I'm certainly not going to suggest that you invest in any particular coin or token.

You, today, are the sum total of the decisions you've made in your life. Many of those decisions were made because you were misled and manipulated. Stop looking for shortcuts. Stop looking for celebrities, rich, or highly educated people to tell you what is best for you. If you continue to do what most people do, you will end up like most people.

Look at the world today. Most people are not well off. Most people are in debt to the banks, hoping they can catch a break and somehow work their way out of the financial mess they are in. This system is rigged to keep you working, spending, and never saving. In short, this system will keep you poor.

When it comes to something that effects your life as much as money, my advice is to learn all you can about it yourself.

Learn from the mistakes of those who came before you. The first part of that is to learn history. British statesman Winston Churchill wrote, **"Those that fail to learn from history are doomed to repeat it."** Those of you who are poor, deep in debt, or who are one step (health, job, accident) from losing everything, this book has told you why. My efforts here hopefully will inspire you to learn more. My challenge to you, as stated at the beginning, is to prove me wrong. As our third president said, **"Knowledge is power."** I would add, **"He who learns last has the least power."** Don't be last. Don't continue to be a victim.

In closing, I thank you for your time, and I remind you that even those who seem financially sound may in fact be living in a financial house of cards. If you have enjoyed or learned anything from this book, please do something to share knowledge of it with others; write a review, talk about it with your friends, family, or anyone you see, or think is struggling with money issues.

About the Author

Jay Dyer was born in 1952 and raised in Southern California. Has been self-employed since the age of 26. After driving a cab for two years, Jay started working in 1975 for an alarm company in Compton, California. The next three years saw Jay working for the top three alarm companies in the state.

In 1978 Jay opened his own alarm company, I D S, which he still has today. He was also a professional photographer from 1976 to 1993, specializing in people. (Modeling, hair, weddings, parties, beauty pageants, portraits, and the like.)

After marrying in 1992, Jay had to give up photography to spend time with his new wife. Fast forward fifteen years…

Jay missed the camera and became an abstract art photographer. He developed a new photo technique that he named DyerLightArt.

Some of his works can be seen at: **deviantart.com/jaydyerlightart** .

In 2015 Jay and his wife Alanda (pronounced Aa-Land-da) started new careers as insurance agents. Alanda still has her own company.

They sold life, health, retirement, and annuities. It was the process of learning about money and the financial world that opened Jay's eyes.

He then discovered Bitcoin. Through it, he also discovered why he and so many people toil most of their lives and end up with little or nothing. In 2016, at the age of 64, Jay learned the true nature of and the real definition of money. He learned the true nature of banking, finance, credit, and debt. Realizing the dollar was rapidly approaching the value of zero, he could not continue down the same path as everyone else.

He learned all he could, then became a crypto manager. He has a small group of people whose purchasing power he has grown many folds in the past three years. Growing future purchasing power for himself and his clients has consumed most of his time until he started writing his first book, "Money, And Bitcoin: Everything You Were Never Taught In School," in 2019.

Jay spends almost all his time on computers, but virtually none on social media. Bitcoin and all the altcoins live on the internet 24/7. Sometimes so does Jay.

Between his alarm company, art, crypto managing, continuing to learn, and his wife, Jay has very little extra time. Jay hopes to fully retire in about five to ten years.

For questions, comments, and to contact Jay, email to: **stwcrypto@1ids.com** .

Made in United States
North Haven, CT
01 May 2024

51979436R00067